Scientists who have changed the world

Galileo Galilei

by Michael White

OTHER TITLES IN THE SERIES
Charles Darwin by Anna Sproule (1-85015-213-6)
Thomas A. Edison by Anna Sproule (1-85015-201-2)
Alexander Fleming by Beverley Birch (1-85015-184-9)
Guglielmo Marconi by Beverley Birch (1-85015-185-7)
Coming soon:
Alexander Graham Bell by Michael Pollard (1-85015-200-4)
Margaret Mead by Anna Sproule (1-85015-228-4)
Isaac Newton by Michael White (1-85015-243-8)
The Wright Brothers by Anna Sproule (1-85015-229-2)

Picture Credits:
Alinari: 36/37; The Bridgeman Art Library: 4; Mary Evans Picture Library: 6, 7, 9 and 10 and 42 (Explorer); Robert Harding Picture Library: 26 (W. Rawlings); Michael Holford: 18, 19 all, 28; Hulton Picture Library: 15; The Image Bank: 5 (W. Bibikow), 27 (P. DeRenzis), 30/31, 58 (C. Place); the Mansell Collection: 20, 43, 56; Photographie Buloz: 54/5; Ann Ronan Picture Library: 8 above, 22, 25, 38 and 39 above and below (Goldschmidt & Co.), 49 above (Royal Astronomical Society), 60 (Goldschmidt & Co.); Scala: cover, 8 below, 12, 13, 16, 33, 44, 48, 51, 59; Science Photo Library: 35 (Dr. H. Edgerton), 41 (NOAO), 45 above and below (NASA), 49 below (Dr. J. Burgess); Weidenfeld & Nicolson Archives: 11, 46, 50, 52/53.

Published in Great Britain in 1991
by Exley Publications Ltd,
16 Chalk Hill, Watford,
Herts WD1 4BN, United Kingdom.

Copyright © Exley Publications, 1991
Copyright © Michael White, 1990

A copy of the CIP data is available from
the British Library on request.

ISBN 1-85015-227-6

Series editor: Helen Exley
Picture research: Elizabeth Loving
Editing: Samantha Armstrong and
  Margaret Montgomery
Typeset by Brush Off Studios, St Albans.
Printed and bound in Hungary.

Galileo Galilei

The story of the brilliant Italian scholar hounded by the Inquisition because of his views on the universe

Michael White

 EXLEY

Opposite: Galileo was put on trial in April 1633 when he was sixty-nine years old. In this picture, you can see him standing in the dock in the corner of the court (top left of picture). Eventually he was forced to retract his views. But, legend has it that, even as he did this, he muttered (of the Earth) "nevertheless it does indeed move!"

Below: Modern astronomy owes a great debt to the work of Galileo. He was one of the great astronomers who laid the foundation for our modern view of the solar system. Today, scientists can probe deep into space and detect radiation from stars millions of light years away from the Earth.

On trial

The court room in the Vatican City in Rome is full. Crammed into the tiers forming a semicircle around the walls are cardinals, bishops, theologians and philosophers. Presiding over the whole affair is the Pope, Urban VIII, leader of the Roman Catholic Church. It is April 1633 and on trial is a sixty-nine-year-old man. He stands in the dock, upright and dignified despite the humiliations he has been put through. His clothes are well-cut but a little unkempt, his hair silver, his face worn and tired.

Despite a severe illness, he has been summoned to Rome. He has had to travel from Florence, through plague-ridden Italy and encroaching winter, because he has angered the Church leaders by claiming that the Earth is not the central point of the Universe. This man is Galileo Galilei, the greatest scientist and mathematician of his age.

In the middle of the massive courtroom sits Pope Urban, the leader of the Roman Catholic Church. Pope Urban has formed powerful political alliances with other countries to halt the progress of Protestantism. He feels that Galileo's work is damaging to the Catholic Church. It could be used against the Catholic religion and, as a result, he has no mercy at all for the man in the dock. For most of the trial his head is bowed in concentration as he listens to the case against Galileo. But, every once in a while, the old man raises his head and frowns at the mathematician. Urban is furious and wants Galileo punished. As far as he is concerned, Galileo has committed one of the worst heresies possible and his teachings have even threatened the Church's authority. For this he should die.

Nicolaus Copernicus, who was born in 1473, nearly a century before Galileo. He had revolutionary views on the nature and movements of the stars and planets and described some of these ideas in short manuscripts during his lifetime. However, a detailed account of his theories was not published until the time of his death in his great work "The Revolution of the Heavenly Spheres". This completely refuted the accepted astronomical ideas of his contemporaries.

To the Pope's left sit his closest servants, the cardinals who head the dreaded Inquisition, the Church's secret police. These men could have Galileo tortured and executed for what he has said and done. They could personally supervise procedings as the old man is stretched on the rack or has burning metal shards thrust under his finger nails. They have done it many times before and would do it again. Thirty-three years earlier in 1600, the Inquisition had ordered the philosopher Giordano Bruno to be burned at the stake for heresy and they have tortured and executed countless others in the intervening years.

Guilty

But, as Galileo faces his most desperate hour, he has one great advantage over any of the other heretics who have faced trial and eventual execution at the hands of the Inquisition. He has gone out of his way to make numerous friends in high places and can count on many of those sitting beside the Pope to come to his aid.

Although many of the powerful men of the Inquisition disagree with Galileo's ideas they understand the complex mind of the great scientist and deep beneath the public image they have to portray, they are desperate to save his life.

During all the agonizing weeks of the trial, as the old man stands in the dock, the Inquisition harangue him with question after question. To all outward appearances they show no mercy with the scientist. As far as the Pope is concerned, his servants are totally devoted to proving Galileo a heretic. He believes wholeheartedly that together they will see him burn.

However, all the while the Inquisition carry out their duty, in private after each day's proceedings over dinner with the Pope, Galileo's friends subtly play down his crimes in an effort to calm the situation and persuade the head of the Church to soften the charges and save the scientist's life.

Each day at the trial, Galileo continues to claim his innocence and to modify his opinions to save

his own life. Then finally, after weeks of inter-rogation and cross-examination, the decisive moment has arrived and the verdict is to be announced.

On the final day of the trial Galileo is brought to the dock for the last time. The court falls silent as the Pope enters and sits down. The representative of the Inquisition strides to the front of the court and opens the document that will seal Galileo's fate. The representative clears his throat and lifts his head. He stares directly at the gathered officials crammed into the courtroom; his voice booms around the room.

Galileo, he pronounces, is guilty and is to be imprisoned for the rest of his life.

"The Dialogue"

The trial of Galileo in 1633 was the climax to a series of events that had begun nearly one hundred years earlier upon the publication of a book called *The Revolution of the Heavenly Spheres*, written by the Polish astronomer, Nicolaus Copernicus. In this book, Copernicus claimed that the Earth was simply a planet orbiting around the Sun. This proposal went totally against the accepted wisdom of the time and was branded as heresy by the Catholic Church.

And here, in the heart of civilized Europe in 1633, we find the most-respected scientist of his generation hauled up in front of the Inquisition. Galileo is accused of the terrible crime of heresy simply because he supports the views suggested in Copernicus's book.

Nine years earlier, Galileo had been asked by Pope Urban VIII to write a book which gave a balanced account of the argument over the nature of the universe. What this really meant was that the Church wanted Galileo to discuss the various arguments, but to finally come down on their side and to disagree with Copernicus. The result of Galileo's work was a book called *Dialogue Concerning the Two Chief Systems of the World*.

The problem was that Galileo did not do as he

Galileo Galilei. Throughout his life he managed to remain on the right side of the dogmatic church establishment – with his scientific genius, quick wit and charisma. It was not until late in life that he came into conflict with the Church by virtue of his support for the heretical views of Nicolaus Copernicus and his open confrontation with the supporters of Aristotle.

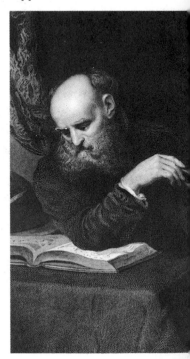

was told. The accepted theories of the universe were based on the idea that the Earth was the central point of the universe. But, in his book Galileo completely destroyed this idea and sided with the heretical Copernicus, stating that the Sun and not the Earth was the central point.

When Urban's advisers received a copy of *The Dialogue* what Galileo had done was immediately obvious and he was summoned to Rome. It is a measure of the Pope's anger that when doctors attending the great scientist protested that he could be moved only at peril to his life, the Pope declared that if he did not come of his own free will, he would be brought in chains.

Above: The front cover of Galileo's "The Dialogue". Below: Pope Urban VIII who was the Pope at the time of Galileo's trial. Here you can see him holding court surrounded by fawning believers.

The Church

Sixteenth century European thought was controlled by two powerful forces: the Roman Catholic Church headed by the Pope, and ancient philosophy dominated by the two-thousand-year-old ideas of the Greek philosopher, Aristotle. The Church had an overwhelming influence on the lives of most Europeans, and this was especially the case with the devoutly Catholic Itâlians. During Galileo's childhood, one in twelve people living in Rome was either a cleric or a nun, which gives some idea of how important a part religion played in public life.

The Catholic Church controlled the people by completely forbidding any teaching that deviated from what was taught in the Bible.

To make sure that this was adhered to, the Church set up the Inquisition, whose job it was to monitor publications and public declarations. Within sympathetic countries they censored books that did not totally agree with traditional Catholic teaching and they tried and prosecuted anyone who persisted in publishing heretical views.

As well as this, the Church set up the Order of Jesuits who worked on scientific problems and taught their version of the truth. Jesuit philosophy and science was what Aristotle had taught. Any discovery made by a Jesuit researcher had to fit

into the accepted, inherited world-view, handed down from Greek times. If an observation did not fit into the scheme of things it had to be false. Aristotle could not be wrong, it was as simple as that. If Aristotle was wrong, by implication so, too, was the Bible, and, despite the fact that this ancient book contains numerous, obvious falsehoods, this idea could never be tolerated.

Aristotle was born in southern Greece in 384 B.C. He was a great thinker and developed theories of how the universe operated two thousand years before the birth of modern science. He had many startlingly accurate ideas about basic science, but was totally wrong about an even greater number.

Aristotle had many misconceptions. He believed that the Moon, along with all other celestial bodies, was featureless and absolutely perfect in form. Instead of suggesting the idea that physical laws worked in the same way throughout the universe,

Copernicus's view of the solar system. Although it is not exactly as astronomers see it today, he was very close to the truth nearly 450 years ago. Copernicus stated that the planets revolved around the Sun and that the Earth was not the central point of the universe. This is called the Heliocentric system. Copernicus also thought that the orbits of the planets were circular, but in 1609 Kepler showed that they were in fact elliptical.

9

he believed that there was one set of physical laws that operated on Earth and a different set for the celestial sphere – the name he gave for anything outside the Earth. He believed that comets were produced inside the Earth's atmosphere and were nothing to do with the celestial sphere.

Above all, the biggest error in Aristotle's thinking was his notion of the Earth's position in space. He believed that the Earth was fixed as the central point of the universe. In Aristotle's philosophy, the Earth did not revolve or move in any way; instead, the Sun, the Moon and all the known planets revolved around the Earth.

Because of mankind's egotistical view of existence, Aristotle's model of the universe was very popular with the Church. After all, Man was made in God's image. It was surely correct, therefore, that the earth should take its rightful place as the central point of the universe.

For two thousand years Aristotle's ideas on all scientific matters had been taught' as irrefutable truth. And, conveniently, his views also happened to coincide with any rare mentions of science in the Bible.

Conflict

This, then, was the state of affairs when, in 1543, Copernicus had stated his theory that in fact the Earth, along with the other planets, revolved around the Sun.

This idea went totally against what Aristotle and the Bible had said. It was considered to be completely false, not because it could be proven by experiment to be false, but simply because it went against what had been taught for two millenia Apart from a few luminaries, such as Copernicus and the German astronomer Johannes Kepler, the scientific world into which Galileo entered when he began work in 1585 was a very sterile place.

Philosophers obsessed with Aristotelian ideas and ignorant of genuine scientific principles, and theologians who took every word in the Bible literally, dominated the intellectual world of southern Europe. If it had not been for the work of men

Johannes Kepler, a contemporary of Galileo's and a great supporter of Copernicus's theories. In 1597, he published a book called "Cosmographic Mystery" which openly upheld the views of Copernicus. He tried to generate Galileo's support for the Copernican, Heliocentric system, but it was not until Galileo lost his temper with the Aristotelians that he publicly came down on the side of Copernicus and Kepler.

such as Galileo, who challenged the accepted wisdom and developed a new way of viewing the world, such ideas could have held back any real scientific advancement in countries like Italy for generations.

The story of Galileo's life is the story of his fight to make the world see that religion should be based on faith and that it should not attempt to answer questions of science. Theologians, he believed, should stick to theology and science should be left to scientists.

Rebellious views

Galileo Galilei was born the eldest child to Vincenzio and Giulia Galilei on February 15, 1564. The family lived in the city of Pisa, situated in the Tuscany region of north-west Italy.

His father, Vincenzio, was a well-known musician who was very interested in musical theory. He became quite famous in Italy as the originator of a number of revolutionary views on music, and was the first person to use mathematics in its study. Galileo himself learned to play the lute while he was still young, and became quite an accomplished musician. Although vivacious and energetic, he enjoyed sitting alone in the courtyard or his room playing the lute or composing his own songs.

As well as being a celebrated musician, Galileo's father gained a reputation as a rebellious thinker. Vincenzio hated closed-minded people, especially those in positions of authority in the academic world. He was forever rebelling against blind acceptance of inherited wisdom. The young Galileo was influenced by some of his father's attitude – in his later work there are definite echoes of his father's anti-establishment opinions. In many ways Galileo argued against narrow-mindedness in the world of science in much the same way that his father had against narrow-mindedness in music.

The era known by historians as the Renaissance began in the Tuscany region where Galileo grew up, about one hundred years before the scientist's birth. It was a time of "re-awakening" in both the

Above: The house near the Porta Fiorentina at Pisa, where Galileo was born on February 15, 1564.

"It appears to me that they who in proof of anything simply rely on the weight of authority, without adducing any argument in support of it, act very absurdly. I, on the contrary, wish to be allowed to raise questions freely and to answer without any adulation of authorities, as becomes those who are truly in search of the truth."

Vincenzio Galilei,
Galileo's father.

11

Sixteenth century Italy was one of the great cultural areas of Europe. It was the birthplace of the Renaissance which blossomed into an era of unprecedented change in the arts and sciences. Here, you can see examples of the great craftsmanship and artistic skill of Italian glass makers.

arts and the sciences. The improvement of printing methods meant an ever increasing number of books was being published. With this came a greater awareness among the public in all the countries of Europe and the ability to communicate ideas and scientific developments more easily.

The mood of the people was one of eagerness for information, for more reality instead of religious symbols, for new discoveries about the planet they lived on, for art and for literature. Where, before the Renaissance, there had been an unquestioning acceptance of medieval ideas, there was now a need for challenge and for knowledge. This was the atmosphere into which Galileo was born and he was to be a true Renaissance man. Not only was he a very versatile thinker, interested in a whole range of subjects, he was above all an open-minded intellectual, always ready to accept new ideas and progressive views. As well as this, he used the latest techniques available to him to communicate his discoveries to others. He published a collection of revolutionary books in his lifetime and did more than any of his contemporaries to push science into a new era.

A monk?

Until the age of eleven, Galileo was educated at home by his father and a series of private tutors. He was a lively, outward-going child who loved to explore and investigate everything around him. When he was not in lessons he would go off on his own to discover secret tunnels and deserted buildings in the city or further afield in the lush countryside of Tuscany.

Tuscany is still a very beautiful place, a land of rich red wines and olive groves. The climate is warm and the summers long. Everywhere is bathed in a mellow orange glow that leaves you with a feeling of peace whether standing in a busy city street or looking out over green fields in the heart of the countryside. In Galileo's day, the area was even more tranquil. There were few roads and no industry. Tuscany must have been close to heaven in the sixteenth century.

Vincenzio Galilei distrusted most educational establishments and strongly resented the thought of sending his eldest son to be indoctrinated at one of them.

In 1575, the family moved to Florence, a large city to the east of Pisa. Of all Italian cities, Florence is considered to be the place where learning and intellectual life was at its greatest. Many historians believe that it was in Florence that the Renaissance began, and when Galileo's family moved there, it was at the pinnacle of its development as the intellectual heart of Europe. Vincenzio could not afford to pay for his son's education so the eleven-year-old Galileo was sent away to a monastery school in the nearby town of Vallombrosa.

However, things there did not run as smoothly as his father hoped. Within three years, Galileo's

A painting of Florence which is part of a fresco by the artist Giorgio Vasari. It was painted about the time Galileo's family moved to the city in 1575 and shows Florence to be a very large, walled city, with sprawling suburbs beyond the river and the fortifications. At the time, Florence was the capital of Tuscany.

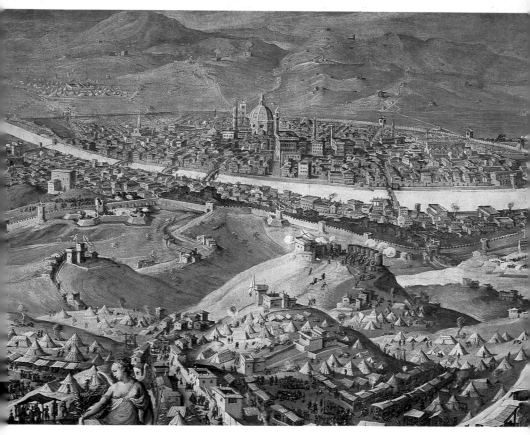

father felt forced to remove him from the school when he discovered that the studious young man had volunteered himself as a novice monk. Vincenzio was horrified by the idea and brought Galileo back to Florence to continue his education.

Conflicts

This incident was to be the first of many conflicts between Galileo and his father. Although they shared views on the rigid and limited outlook of the academic world, they disagreed on the best course for Galileo's career.

In 1581, when he was seventeen, Galileo was enrolled at the University of Pisa, the town where he had been born. His father insisted that he study medicine as this was seen to be the best first step on the ladder to success and eventual riches for an academic in sixteenth-century Italy.

Galileo reluctantly went along with his father's wishes, but within a few months, further conflicts began to brew. Galileo was a multi-talented young man. He was a gifted musician, an excellent painter and an extremely good writer. But, it was while in his first year at Pisa that his lack of interest in medicine and the discovery of his real love changed the course of his life.

During his first term at Pisa University, Galileo began attending mathematics lectures in his spare time and had become captivated by the stark beauty of the subject. In particular, he was fascinated by lectures, delivered by the court mathematician Ostillo Ricci, on the subject of Euclidean geometry – the branch of mathematics named after the Greek, Euclid, who was the father of geometry.

Galileo attended Ricci's lectures week after week. Before long, the court mathematician began to notice a well-built, handsome young man who always sat at the back of the lecture hall, listening intently to his every word. At the end of each talk Galileo would ask Ricci innumerable searching questions. The mathematician realized that he had a very talented student at his lectures and encouraged him to study mathematics rather than medicine at the university.

Despite his father's anger, Galileo went ahead and changed courses. He was no longer a child, he insisted, and would not go along with his father's demands this time. By the end of the first term, Galileo was a mathematics undergraduate.

"The Wrangler"

It was at the University of Pisa that Galileo's impatience with the attitudes of philosophers to science came to the fore in arguments and private discussions. On many occasions, he would become heated and raise his voice, loudly disputing the views of his colleagues and lecturers.

Galileo undoubtedly had a mischievous streak, but he was basically a respectful and well-disciplined student. He was well-liked by the other students and gained quite a reputation for his quick wit and cheekiness. However, when it came to questions of mathematics and physics, he had no fears about making his views very clear. In fact, he argued so much at university that he got himself the nickname *Il Attaccabrighe*, "The Wrangler".

His main argument was that science could never progress by just sitting and thinking about it in the way the Greeks had done. Aristotle had not

Pisa, where Galileo attended the University as a student between 1581 and 1585 and again as a professor between 1589 and 1592. Despite enjoying some of his childhood in the city before the Galilei family moved to Florence, he was never really happy at the University. He came into conflict with his superiors on a number of matters, both as a student and as a teacher.

conducted a single experiment in his entire life. He reached conclusions simply by a process of applying logic. And that, Galileo argued, was not all. Aristotle's entire system was interconnected, óne principle led to another and each idea supported the others. If one part of his philosophy was wrong, it could all be brought into question.

Galileo's approach was the opposite to Aristotle's. At Pisa he argued that science could only be based on experiment. An idea might well be based on inspiration at first, but it could only be proven and accepted by experiment – a view that is taken for granted today.

Most of Galileo's colleagues at the university disagreed with his views. Knowing the Church's attitude, Galileo was wise enough to argue his view as being merely one of many suggestions and gave no more weight to his anti-Aristotelian thoughts than any others. That, at least, was his approach in public....

Opposite: One Sunday in 1583 Galileo made his first important scientific discovery. During a rather boring sermon he watched one of the church lamps gently swinging. This led him to carry out further experiments to investigate the motion of a pendulum. Based on this work, Galileo formulated a law describing the pendulum swing. Later these ideas were used in the construction of the first accurate clocks.

The pendulum swing

Galileo made his first important scientific discovery while still at the University of Pisa. And, ironically, it was all thanks to the Church.

Although in later life Galileo would come into serious conflict with the Church, throughout his life he was a devout Catholic and attended mass at Pisa Cathedral every Sunday. On one such Sunday in 1583, he donned his best gown and walked to church through the cobbled streets already busy with fellow church-goers.

As fate would have it, on this particular Sunday the service was taken by a visiting priest who delivered a very dull sermon. Before long, Galileo became bored and his eyes began to wander around the great vaulting ceiling of the cathedral. It was then that he spotted, high overhead, a swinging lamp. After a few moments he became mesmerized by the hypnotic rhythm of the lamp's seductive motion. Suddenly a thought struck him. He had seen objects swinging many times before, but had never realized a startling fact about them.

Sometimes the distance the lamp swung would be shorter, sometimes longer as it was moved by the air currents in the cathedral. However, no matter what the distance was, the lamp always seemed to take the same amount of time to complete one swing.

He had no timepiece or clock of any kind with which to measure the exact time of the swing, so he checked the time with his own pulse as he had done with many experiments at the university.

Before the boring sermon was over, the truth was clear to see: each swing took the same length of time to go from one end of its path to the other. This occurred if the lamp went through a long swing, when buffeted by a gust of air, or a small swing.

After mass, Galileo rushed back to his quarters at the university and began to experiment with a number of home-made copies of the lamp by attaching weights to lengths of string. Again he timed the swings as carefully as he could with the only timepiece available – his own pulse. Although this method of measuring the passage of time was not totally accurate, it showed quite clearly that his original notion had been correct.

Galileo had discovered the pendulum, and stated the simple law that "whatever the length of a pendulum swing, the time taken to complete the swing is the same". Scientists call this the pendulum's periodic swing.

Above: A sandglass, one of the ways of measuring time before Galileo's discoveries.
Opposite: Top left: The basic framework of a pendulum clock, designed by Galileo in the last years of his life. Top right: One of the world's earliest clocks, built about fifty years after Galileo's death and constructed on the principles he had first put forward. Below: A sundial that tells the time by observing the shadow cast across its face by the sunlight falling on a string. This type of sundial was a portable, but not very accurate, predecessor of the watch.

The first accurate clock

After making this discovery, Galileo decided to pursue the matter further. He made a huge variety of pendulums using different weights or "bobs", changing the length of the string, changing the shape of the bob as well as the type of string it was attached to. Noting down the results of his experiments, he then began to look for patterns in the data. Gradually a number of simple laws became apparent.

First, he discovered that the period – or length of time – of the swing was not affected at all by the weight of the bob. If the same length of string

was used and only the weight of the bob was changed, the periodic time was the same.

Next, by using the same bob but using different lengths of string, Galileo saw that the length of string was a crucial factor. In fact, after repeating the experiment a number of times a very clear relationship began to emerge. The time needed to complete a swing depended only on the square root of the length of the string.

Galileo could not really explain why this rule applied. In fact it was not until the next century when much more was known about gravity and forces acting on objects that an explanation was found. In the sixteenth century, scientists simply did not have the mathematical knowledge to give a satisfactory explanation about the way the pendulum behaved.

However, Galileo was quick to realize that his new discovery had a number of applications. His

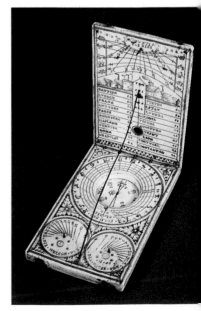

first suggestion was to use pendulums to construct an accurate clock.

Until the sixteenth century, scientists had serious difficulties measuring short time periods. Galileo himself was becoming increasingly frustrated with the inaccurate machines available and he often had to rely on very inferior ways of measuring time periods. Unbelievably, his method of using his own pulse was more accurate than any manufactured timepiece of the day.

Eventually, near the end of Galileo's life, the idea of using pendulums in clocks was accepted. But, the discoverer himself gained nothing from it. It seems strange that he did not try to make more of the idea at the time. Perhaps he did not realize its full commercial potential, or was distracted by other happenings in his busy life, for Galileo was never short of ideas and as it would turn out a more dramatic event was about to take place.

The end of student life

Aged twenty-one, Galileo left university in 1585 without obtaining a degree. Although this seems strange after four years of study, it was quite common in sixteenth century Italy, where official qualifications were not as important as one's reputation in academic circles.

Galileo moved back to the district where his family lived between Florence and Siena. Once he had settled in, he immediately set about trying to earn a living. His father could no longer support him and he had only his mathematical skills and university experience to rely on.

Galileo was a very likeable young man and had a winning charm. This would not be the last time in his life that his open friendliness would be a great asset to him. Shortly after arriving he went out of his way to make friends with a number of wealthy families in the area and let it be known that he was willing to teach science to their children, or indeed to anyone interested and willing to pay for his services. Sometimes Galileo would have to travel for several hours to reach the beautiful villas of

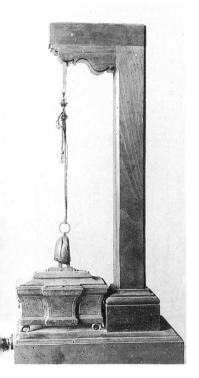

The actual pendulum used by Galileo in his experiments, conducted after seeing the lamp's motion in the church. After carrying out numerous experiments and altering all the variables, he could state with certainty, the law which says that "whatever the length of a pendulum swing, the time taken to complete the swing is the same."

of some of his colleagues.

It was not only at the university that his outspoken views were beginning to make him enemies. He severely and publicly criticized a scheme to dredge a nearby port that would have made a great deal of money for a local property developer. This businessman, it turned out, was a good friend of the head of the university.

Some good things eventually came from Galileo's actions.

The continued refusal of his scientific colleagues to let go of their outmoded Aristotelian attitudes encouraged Galileo to do some of his most important work in physics – partly as an act of rebellion. In particular, he was growing increasingly angry with his associates' refusal to accept that Aristotle was wrong on the question of what happened to objects when they were allowed to fall from rest.

In 1590, he brought together all of his developing ideas on motion and falling bodies in a book called *De Motu,* "On Motion".

"De Motu"

De Motu cannot be called a great work of science. A number of ideas suggested by Galileo were not fully developed at the time of writing, and in places the text is a strange blend of science and imagination. Galileo realized this soon after it was completed. He was particularly self-critical over the fact that, at times, he had been breaking his own "golden rule" and had not supported his "ideas" with real experimental evidence.

Just as the book was about to go to press, he withdrew the manuscript and it was only published in a far more developed form many years later.

One of the basic principles in *De Motu* was to do with the theory of falling objects.

Aristotle had stated that objects of different weight fell at different speeds. Galileo was convinced that this idea was completely wrong. Instead, he believed that all objects fell at the same speed regardless of their weight.

This was not an original idea; other scientists had suggested it before. In particular the Flemish

An engraving made from a classical bust of the Greek philosopher Aristotle. Aristotle was born nearly four hundred years before Christ and, although he is recognized as one of the great thinkers of history, he got many things wrong. He had ideas that would appear quite bizarre to a modern scientist. Despite this, the word of Aristotle was taken as absolute truth for nearly two thousand years.

engineer Simon Stevin, a contemporary of Galileo's, had conducted experiments on falling lead weights and written an account of his work.

Galileo's conviction caused a number of arguments with his colleagues at the university, who were equally convinced that Aristotle's view was correct.

Not long after Galileo withdrew his book, these arguments came to a head and he made the decision to produce a clear and totally convincing demonstration to show that the Greek philosopher had been wrong. What followed was to become one of the most famous incidents in the history of science.

The Leaning Tower of Pisa

There were many famous incidents in Galileo's long life, remembered and recorded by later generations. Probably the most popular story is one involving an experiment he is said to have conducted from the top of the Leaning Tower of Pisa in 1591.

In Pisa city there stands the Leaning Tower. This extraordinary building was built in 1174 and from its earliest times it began to lean until it is now some seventeen feet out of the perpendicular. By the sixteenth century, the Leaning Tower of Pisa had become a landmark that attracted the attention of visitors from all over Italy.

So angry had Galileo become with the beliefs of his colleagues, who adamantly refused to even consider his anti-Aristotelian ideas, that he decided to prove the Greek philosopher wrong with a spectacular demonstration.

One of Aristotle's fundamental ideas in physics was that if two objects of different weight were allowed to fall under the influence of gravity, the heavier one of the two would reach the ground first. But, as with all his propositions, Aristotle never tested the concepts with experiments and it was merely accepted as undeniable fact.

To prove his point, Galileo climbed to the top of the Leaning Tower with two assistants and two cannon-balls of different weights.

The climb was nerve-racking. To reach the top

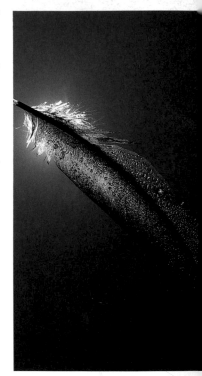

Opposite: The Leaning Tower of Pisa.

Above: Aristotle stated that objects of different weights fell at different speeds. Galileo showed that this was false by dropping two different weights from the top of the Leaning Tower of Pisa. If he had used a lead weight and a feather in the experiment, the lead weight would indeed have landed long before the feather. This is not because of their different weights, but because the feather experiences far greater air resistance than the lead weight. Air resistance slows objects down.

In 1642, Robert Boyle demonstrated that the only force that slows objects in free fall is air resistance. To show this, he used this apparatus. He found that if the air was completely removed from the glass jar then objects as different as a feather and a lead bullet took the same time to fall the height of the jar.

of the Leaning Tower he had to climb hundreds of worn and slippery steps, winding round in a steep spiral staircase inside the stone walls. By the time he reached the top, he was sweating and weary. But, he had a job to do. Spurred on by his anger and frustration, he climbed on to the bell tower high above the upper platform of the tower. It leaned to one side at a frightening angle. He only just managed to submerge his feelings of vertigo and pressed on to the highest point. He had never stood on such a high building before.

He positioned himself at the edge of the bell tower with the two cannon-balls, 179 feet above the ground. He looked out over Pisa. At the base of the tower he could see his doubting colleagues from the university whom he had persuaded to attend. He stretched out his hand to test for any breeze. It was calm.

The two assistants leaned over the edge. Each held a cannon-ball. At the appropriate moment, Galileo gave the signal. The assistants let go of the balls at the same instant allowing them to fall under the force of gravity to the grass below.

Sure enough, it was clearly seen that both balls reached the ground at almost the same time, proving beyond any doubt that Aristotle had been completely wrong.

Farewell to Pisa

This simple experiment showed that what Galileo Galilei and others had said was true. The only force that could alter the speed of fall was air resistance. Objects with large surface areas were slowed more than those with compact ones.

In fact it would be fifty years later, soon after Galileo's death in 1642, that the Irish scientist Robert Boyle would conduct an experiment that confirmed Galileo's theory.

Boyle pumped all the air out of a glass jar and allowed a lead bullet and a feather to fall the height of the jar under the influence of gravity. He found that the bullet and the feather reached the base of the jar simultaneously.

However, Galileo's success was followed by disappointment. He began to hear reports that his contract at the university would not be renewed when the three-year term was completed.

Then, tragedy struck. In the winter of 1591, his father Vincenzio died unexpectedly, leaving the twenty-seven-year-old Galileo as the head of the family and responsible for their welfare.

Worse still was the fact that, before his death, Vincenzio had promised a large dowry to Galileo's sister Virginia.

During his life Vincenzio Galilei had constantly lost any money he had made from music by backing ambitious business projects and unprofitable ideas that repeatedly failed. Consequently, when he died, the Galileis were suddenly pushed to the edge of financial ruin. As the eldest son, the burden of sorting out the family's affairs fell on Galileo's shoulders.

More troubles lay ahead. Within weeks of his father's death and with financial problems mounting, Galileo's contract at the university came up for renewal. He had created enemies with both his satirical literature and his ideas for the dredging of the local port. Not only that, but his anti-Aristotelian opinions had turned his superiors against him. He held out little hope that the university authorities would be sympathetic to his family's problems.

As he had feared, the request for renewal of his contract was turned down by the university and the twenty-seven-year-old professor was asked to seek alternative employment.

Just at the point when all seemed lost, Galileo's friend the Marquis del Monte came to the rescue again and helped him secure a post as Professor of Mathematics at the far more liberal University of Padua.

By early 1592, Galileo had moved to Padua and taken up his new job at the university with a salary three times larger than he had received in his previous position.

Now he was able to support his mother, brothers and sisters and start to pay off the promised dowry.

"Galileo Galilei not only relished his battles with the Church, but also enjoyed quarrelling with the latter-day Aristotelians, heirs to the ancient science handed down through Islamic culture, to the Middle Ages. Galileo pictured himself as a heroic protagonist of 'The New Science' against the dogmatic absurdities of the 'Old Science'."
Colin Ronan, from "Man Masters Nature".

"Galileo thought that all he had to do was to show that Copernicus was right, and everybody would listen. That was his first mistake: the mistake of being naive about people's motives."
J. Bronowski, from "The Ascent of Man".

Galileo moved to the city of Padua in north-eastern Italy in 1592. He was appointed as Professor of Mathematics at the University – thanks to the influence of his friend the Marquis del Monte. Galileo felt much happier working at the more liberal University of Padua than he had been at the University of Pisa.

Padua

In the sixteenth century, Italy was divided into a number of independent states. Although each state had its own ruler, they were all joined in an alliance under the leadership of Rome. Padua, a city situated in the north-east of the country, came under the sovereignty of Venice, twenty miles away on the coast. Venice was governed by a progressive noble family and was internationally famous for its enlightened court. Consequently, the University of Padua was a haven for radical thinkers like Galileo.

Academic groups had sprung up outside the university and among the intellectuals of the district where discussion of unconventional ideas was actively encouraged.

By this time, Galileo had made quite a name for himself as an anti-Aristotelian thinker and radical

mathematician. Upon his arrival he was welcomed with open arms by the intellectuals of Padua.

As he had grown older, Galileo had lost none of his charm and easy-going nature and very soon he made friends with a number of respected gentlemen and philosophers in the city. He struck up a particularly close friendship with a rich nobleman named Gianvincenzo Pinelli. Pinelli was the embodiment of the Renaissance. He was a man of great wealth and an insatiable desire for knowledge. He owned a magnificent house in the city and a library containing over eighty thousand volumes, making it one of the best in sixteenth century Europe.

When Galileo first arrived in Padua, he lodged with his rich friend while the university arranged suitable accommodation for their new professor.

The great advantage with this arrangement was that Galileo had daily, uninterrupted use of Pinelli's extraordinary library.

Through his friendship with Pinelli, Galileo was invited to join the Pinelli Circle which was sponsored by his nobleman friend and was the most influential of the Paduan societies.

Galileo became an important and respected member of the society very quickly. The members held regular meetings and weekly debates on scientific and philosophical matters. In fact the Pinelli Circle became so prestigious that some members came from other states to attend meetings.

It was during his time at Pinelli's house that Galileo met many men who were to play very important roles in his life. But, perhaps there was none more important than a number of senior men drawn to Pinelli's famous meetings whilst on business trips in Padua. Galileo met them at his companion's house on a number of occasions and became friendly with several of them. These men were one day to become leaders of the Inquisition.

Galileo's true love

Life at the University of Padua suited Galileo, but despite earning a larger salary, supporting his family proved difficult and he had to take private students as he had done in Pisa.

By working long hours he gradually built up a healthy business, teaching mechanics to military engineers based in the city as well as giving astronomy and mathematics lessons to local enthusiasts.

Over the years, things gradually improved and Galileo was able to buy a small house in the city. He began a relationship with a Venetian woman named Marina Gamba. The couple did not marry, but lived together for more than a decade, parting in 1610 when Galileo moved once again and left Marina in Padua. In the years they were together the couple had two daughters and a son.

Galileo showed little interest in marrying Marina and seems to have become increasingly preoccupied with his researches as he got older. He never failed

to provide for all those who depended on him but he could never be considered a loving parent or devoted partner. He really only had one true love in his life – science.

This eighteen-year period in Padua was the happiest of Galileo's life and it was also the time in which he made some of his most important discoveries.

The inclined plane

What he had shown with the Leaning Tower experiment in Pisa was that all objects fall equal distances in equal times, irrespective of their weight. But, his famous demonstration showed nothing about how they fell or whether they changed speed during the descent.

Once again the fact that there were no accurate clocks available caused a problem. Unless an object was allowed to fall from an extremely high altitude,

Galileo made important friends during the eighteen years he spent living in Padua. Many of his greatest discoveries were made while at the University. It was probably the happiest period of his life, a time during which he took a mistress, Marina Gamba, and fathered three children by her. Life in this progressive-thinking city suited his unorthodox attitudes to science and nature.

it took a relatively short time to reach the ground. The method of timing using the pulse was practically useless for such experiments.

People are often surprised that Galileo did not turn back to his earlier ideas for constructing an accurate pendulum clock at this point. The answer is probably that it would have meant too much of a distraction and that he wanted to work out a simple, quick way of measuring time periods just to use in solving the immediate problem. Very soon he did just that.

Timing

Instead of releasing an object from a height and allowing it to fall freely, he thought of repeating the experiment by allowing balls to roll down a specially-designed chute inclined at an angle. This had the effect of slowing the descent considerably without altering the basic motion of the ball. It was still falling under gravity and if the effect of friction was ignored, the motion matched the movements of a cannon-ball dropped from the Leaning Tower of Pisa.

The ball took far longer to reach the end of the chute than it did falling from a height, and by lowering the chute to produce a small angle with the horizontal, it could be made to move at a speed easily measured by yet another cunning device.

Instead of measuring his pulse, Galileo set up a large barrel of water next to the experiment. At the base of the barrel a tiny hole was made that allowed the contents to empty gradually. He repeated the experiment many times and measured the quantity of water collected in a bucket beneath the barrel.

Next, he altered the distance that the ball moved, starting the journey at different points along the chute, and repeating the experiment using longer and longer journeys.

In time, a clear pattern began to emerge, a pattern to which a simple mathematical formula could be fitted. A pattern that led to the idea of acceleration.

Acceleration

When objects travel at a constant speed, they cover equal distances in equal times. You experience this if you cruise along the street at a constant speed in a car. It is only when objects speed up that they experience an acceleration.

Now, it could have been that in Galileo's Leaning Tower experiment, the cannon-balls were falling at a constant speed. That would have meant that they had suddenly reached a steady and unchanging speed straight after leaving the assistants' hands. This was obviously absurd. So, the only other possibility, it seemed to Galileo, was that falling objects gradually gained speed as they fell from rest. In other words, they accelerated.

To prove this, he set up the chute experiment and repeated the process of allowing a ball to roll different distances and timing the length of the journey.

In the first experiment, the ball was allowed to travel eight feet. This took two time units as measured by the dripping water. Next the ball was allowed to roll eighteen feet. It was found to take three time units. Finally, the ball was allowed to travel thirty-two feet along the chute. The journey took four time units. At once Galileo saw a pattern.

The difference in distance between the first and second experiment was ten feet (eighteen minus eight), yet the ball covered this last ten feet in the same time it took to travel eight feet in the first experiment. In the third experiment, the ball went fourteen feet further than in the second experiment (thirty-two minus eighteen), and yet it did this in the same time as it took to travel eight feet in the first experiment and ten feet in the second – one time unit.

So, it seemed obvious that the further the ball went, the greater its final speed. As it fell, the ball went faster and faster – or in other words it accelerated.

If this seems difficult to believe, think about what the average speed of each ball would be at the end of each experiment.

In this high speed photograph you can see a juggler juggling five baseballs. In order to maintain this smooth movement, he has to overcome the force of gravity pulling the balls to the Earth. He manages this by making them accelerate upward using the force produced by the muscles in his arms. If the upward acceleration is too great, the balls will climb too high. If the acceleration against gravity is not large enough, the balls will not rise very high above his hands.

The average speed can be easily calculated by dividing the distance the ball rolled by the time taken for the journey.

So for instance, in the first experiment, when the ball rolled a distance of eight feet in two time units, its average speed by the end of its journey was four feet per time unit ($8 \div 2 = 4$). In the second experiment, the ball would have an average speed of $18 \div 3$ or six feet per time unit, and in the third experiment, where the ball covered a distance of thirty-two feet, the speed would be eight feet per time unit.

So, what this experiment clearly showed was that the only thing to affect the time taken for the ball's journey either along a slope or falling vertically, was the distance it fell. If two objects, whatever their weight, were allowed to fall or roll equal distances along the chute they would arrive at the end of their journey at the same time.

Ballistics

Galileo's discoveries caused quite a stir in the scientific world. He described his findings in detail in notebooks and sent a long letter detailing the

Galileo's Leaning Tower experiment demonstrated that Aristotle had been wrong about falling objects. But, it was only when Galileo devised the idea of using an inclined plane to measure the time interval of a ball's fall that he could obtain quantitative results. In this picture, Galileo is seen demonstrating his experiment. The Leaning Tower can be seen in the background implying that the incident occurred in Pisa, but this could easily be attributed to the imagination of the nineteenth century artist who painted it.

experiments to a good friend from the Pinelli Circle – the Venetian physicist Paolo Sarpi.

At this time Galileo was earning extra income from designing and selling mechanical calculating devices to Venetian military leaders. It was through this contact that he became interested in the subject of ballistics, the study of projectiles. However, once again Galileo found himself conflicting with the accepted ideas of the time.

Conventional physics stated that only one force could act on an object at any one instant, but Galileo was able to destroy this idea by performing a simple "thought experiment". This is an experiment performed only in the scientist's mind, in which the process is described in detail, but is never actually performed.

Galileo pointed out that if a ball was dropped from the top of a ship's mast, the ball landed at the base of the mast and not halfway along the deck, yet the ship itself was moving. Obviously, the ball was experiencing the same motion as the ship. So, not only was the ball acted upon by the force of gravity as it fell from the top of the mast, but it was also experiencing the same forward motion as the ship.

Above and opposite top: Two drawings made before Galileo's birth, showing how Aristotle's ideas were employed in warfare. Aristotle thought that a cannonball simply flew in two straight lines and dropped out of the sky above the target. Opposite: The correct representation of a cannonball's path. This picture appeared in Galileo's "Discourses Upon Two New Sciences" in 1638 and shows cannonballs moving in parabolas and experiencing both the initial thrust and the force of gravity during their flight.

It was clear that Galileo was right again. People had sailed the seas for thousands of years and no one had ever experienced an object landing a long way from the mast when dropped directly down.

Cannon-balls

Galileo went on to use this idea to explain the motions of a projectile fired from a cannon.

He began by stating that the ball is acted upon by two forces – gravity and the initial impetus from the explosion inside the cannon.

He showed that, if the force of gravity is ignored for a moment, then the explosion alone caused the cannon-ball to travel with a constant velocity. The fact that the cannon-ball was moving with a constant speed was obvious since the explosion inside the cannon only occurred once and produced no further boosts of energy. But, from his free fall experiments, Galileo knew that the cannon-

ball would also accelerate toward the Earth due to gravity.

By careful experiment, he showed that the result of these two actions on the ball was to send it along

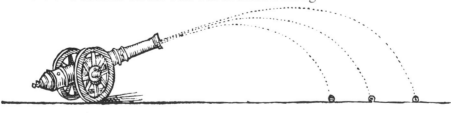

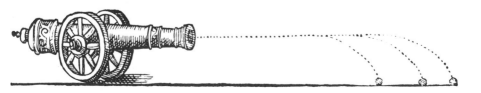

an arched pathway called a parabola. This curve bent away from the originally-straight course out of the mouth of the cannon and toward the Earth. As well as this, by repeating his experiments hundreds of times, Galileo showed that the greatest range could be obtained if the cannon was angled at forty-five degrees to the horizontal.

Meanwhile, further blows to Aristotle's description of the universe were on the horizon.

In 1597, the German scientist Johannes Kepler published a book called *Mysterium Cosmographicum* or "Cosmographic Mystery" which openly supported Copernicus's view of the universe. The book was based on the concept of a universe with the planets – including the Earth – revolving around the Sun.

Kepler knew of Galileo's work and thought that he may be able to lend support to the anti-Aristotelian cause. He sent a copy of his manuscript to Galileo. Some time later the Italian scientist wrote to his German colleague praising his work and siding with his revolutionary theories. But when, a few months later, Johannes Kepler wrote back and asked him to announce his support publicly, Galileo did not reply and let the matter slide.

Some see this as a rather hypocritical thing to do. But, from a position of religious freedom, it is easy to criticize without knowing all the facts.

The truth is that Kepler was living in Germany, a long way from the influence and power of the tyrannical Roman Catholic Church, and its misguided, but all-encompassing, rule. In Padua, Galileo was on Rome's doorstep, in the very heartland of extremist ferment. At that time he was not prepared to go the whole way and announce his views publicly.

Supernova

Seven years later, in 1604, a rare astronomical event occurred which again sent ripples through the scientific community – a supernova appeared in the night sky, outshining everything but the Moon.

A supernova is really an exploding star and they have only been recorded on a few occasions. Of

course, no one in 1604 knew what had caused the supernova, but that was not important. What was significant was that it had happened at all.

Aristotle had stated that the universe was constant and unchanging. But, if that was the case, what was this strange object that had suddenly appeared in the sky?

Once again, Aristotle's two-thousand-year-old ideas were under attack by an observable event. The appearance of the supernova was yet another nail in the coffin of Greek philosophy. But, despite this, there was still resistance to the new revolutionary ideas of Galileo and his supporters.

A supernova. This was photographed in 1987 and was the brightest observed supernova since the one seen by Galileo nearly four hundred years ago. It was the observation of this event in 1604 that sparked off further controversy over the accepted Aristotelian view of astronomy and brought Galileo into conflict with conventional astronomers of the day.

The telescope

In July 1609, when Galileo was forty-five years old, he went to visit his friend Paolo Sarpi in Venice. While he was there, Sarpi mentioned that he had

The Dutch optician, Hans Lipperhey, who is credited with inventing the earliest form of telescope. In October 1608, he applied to the Dutch government for a patent to allow him to be the sole manufacturer of the instrument. Less than a year later, a telescope had arrived in Padua and Galileo heard that telescopes were on sale in Paris.

heard through his foreign contacts that a Dutch spectacle-maker, Hans Lipperhey, had invented an instrument he called a telescope. Sarpi briefly described the device as being made by placing two lenses at opposite ends of a tube. When directed at a distant object, a magnified image could be seen by placing one end of the tube to the eye and looking through the two lenses.

When he returned to Padua, Galileo set about designing and constructing his own version.

Before long, a number of different telescope designs began to appear in scientific circles. Most of these were imported from other parts of Europe and all were of very poor quality, giving a fuzzy image and very low magnification.

Most people saw these telescopes as mere novelties and cared little for their quality. Galileo set his mind to radically improving these toys. He was determined to produce a usable scientific instrument.

He ground his own lenses to a highly-polished finish and masked off the front lens of the telescope so that light could not pass through its extreme edges and distort the image. By making these fairly simple modifications he was able to greatly improve the magnifying power of the device and to produce a far clearer image.

A golden opportunity

Galileo's improvements came just at the right time. In August 1609, Sarpi heard that the ruler of the Venetian state, the Doge of Venice, had been offered a telescope at a very high price by a foreign designer.

Sarpi had heard of the offer when the Doge had come to him for advice on the matter. When Sarpi discovered what a poor image the telescope produced and that it only magnified three times, he immediately advised against buying it. Instead, knowing that his friend Galileo had been making advances in the design of his own telescope, he persuaded the rich Venetian ruler to buy Galileo's instrument.

Galileo had indeed been making great advances. While most available telescopes were barely producing three times the magnification, Galileo had obtained magnifications of nine times.

Galileo's device was obviously of great use to the Doge. Venice was a maritime state that protected a small empire in the Adriatic Sea. A telescope of this type could have immense military use.

With Sarpi's influence, the Doge made Galileo the offer of a lifetime. He would take the telescope and, in exchange, give Galileo a permanent, lifelong post at the University of Padua and a massive pay rise quite unheard of for a mathematician.

Although this may seem an irresistible offer, Galileo was not totally convinced.

On the one hand he was very comfortable in Padua, he was happy with Marina and the children enjoyed living in the city. But, there were other things to consider. He felt restless. He needed to live and work in a larger city. The University of Padua was well-respected, but he needed greater support for his work at a bigger university. The world was opening up, communications were improving all the time and he wanted his work to reach a wider public. He wanted greater recognition. What was more, he had grown tired of teaching at the University. He wanted more time for his researches and resented wasting it on his teaching commitments.

However, the Doge's offer was exceptional, and there were no others to compete with it. After much deliberation Galileo decided to accept the terms of the agreement and prepared the latest model of his telescope to hand over to its new owner.

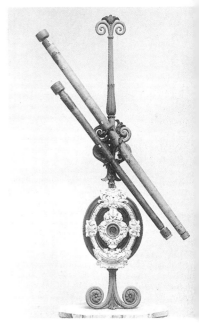

Two telescopes designed and built by Galileo. Both are now preserved in Florence. The earlier telescopes to go on sale probably magnified no more than a factor of two, but Galileo's telescopes were far more sophisticated than any others made at the time. The larger of the two has a magnification of fourteen and the smaller, a magnification of twenty.

Shifting allegiances

Unfortunately, all did not go according to plan.

The contract of agreement from the Doge of Venice was totally different to the verbal promises he had made. The pay rise was nothing like the one promised and there were a number of unpleasant conditions written into the contract which Galileo had no desire to agree to. If he agreed to

Through his friend, Paolo Sarpi, Galileo heard that the Doge of Venice was on the verge of buying an inferior telescope to the ones he was currently making. Galileo managed to convince the ruler that he would be wiser to make him an offer for his latest device. However, the deal presented by the Doge turned out to be less than satisfactory.

the terms, he would forfeit any future pay rises and would have had to lecture on a regular basis until he retired.

Galileo was furious and immediately began to look elsewhere for a new position. He had heard that the post of court mathematician at Florence had become vacant. Without wasting any time, he made a hasty visit to show off his latest telescope to the ruler of Florence, the Grand Duke Cosimo.

After a series of dramatic demonstrations of the telesope's power, Cosimo was convinced. This amazing device was the greatest invention of mortal man, and its creator was offering his services at a very reasonable price. Within twenty-four hours of his arrival at the Florentine court, Cosimo had acquired thc talents of this great man, Galileo. The scientist would move there as soon as possible.

Back in Padua, Galileo continued experimenting with the wonderful new device. There was much to discover.

The first thing he studied through his telescope was the Moon. And, as was happening more and more frequently these days, straight away he ran into conflicts with Aristotle's theories.

Aristotle had stated that the Moon was a perfect and unblemished sphere, but even a casual observation with a telescope revealed craters and crevices covering the entire surface. Worse was to come. On the first night of observation it became abundantly clear that there were even more impressive objects on the moon's surface. Everywhere Galileo looked, between the craters and crevices were nothing less than towering mountains!

Galileo was able to calculate the heights of the Moon's mountains by measuring the length of shadows they cast on the surface. It was then that he received the greatest shock of all. He found that some of them were taller than known mountains on Earth!

After months spent studying the Moon, Galileo turned his telescope to the planets, and in early 1610, he made one of his greatest discoveries.

Night after night, he observed black dots set against the bright surface of the planet Jupiter. The strange thing was, these black dots were moving at a steady pace. Then, one night soon after he had made his first observation, he turned his telescope toward the distant planet only to find that some of the black dots had disappeared.

At first he thought that the dots were a strange effect produced by light reflecting inside the telescope barrel. But, by carrying out careful tests and eliminating all possible problems with the telescope itself, he was forced to come to the only possible conclusion. Jupiter had moons that orbited the giant planet in the same way that our single Moon orbits the Earth.

Venus

It was not until September 1610 that forty-six-year-old Galileo finally managed to arrange the move to Florence. Within a few days of settling into his new home, he was working with his telescope again. It was then that he made a further monumental

Photographs of the moons of Jupiter taken by the Voyager spacecraft. Galileo could only see four moons with his telescope, but there are at least eight more moons.

discovery, a discovery that would push him a step further into the troubles ahead.

He began to make observations of the planet Venus and very gradually a remarkable thing began to reveal itself. By observing the planet every night for several months, he realized that Venus had phases.

From the Earth, the Moon appears to shrink and grow again during the month it takes to orbit the Earth. These are called the phases of the Moon and people had been observing them since earliest times.

Like all planets and their satellites, the Moon does not produce light of its own. It can only reflect the light of the Sun. So, as the Moon passes between the Earth and the Sun we cannot see it because all the light landing on the Sun side is reflected away from us, back in the direction of the Sun. Gradually, as the Moon moved around the Earth, more and more light is reflected our way and we see more and more of the Moon until it reaches what we call Full Moon. At this point, the Moon appears as a full bright circle, reflecting the light from the Sun directly to the Earth.

As Galileo's fame spread he was frequently invited by the nobility of Europe to give lectures and public demonstrations of his telescope. This is the Villa Medici, the Florentine embassy in Rome. Because Italy was divided up into separate states, there were embassies in each state very much like those in different nations today. Galileo stayed at the Villa Medici whenever he visited Rome.

If Venus also had phases, said the Aristotelians, then surely this was proof that it revolved around the Earth just like the Moon. Once again, they were to be proven wrong.

Galileo observed the planet for several months and found that the phases of Venus were far longer than those of the Moon. Whereas the Moon goes through all its phases in one month, Venus takes nearly one-and-a-half years to complete the cycle! This, of course, would mean that the orbit of Venus around the Earth would be far, far larger than was conceived by Aristotle.

A far simpler explanation was that Venus was nearer to the Sun than the Earth and orbited the Sun just like our planet. At one stage in its journey, it lies between the Earth and the Sun and we cannot see it at all because we receive no reflected light from its surface. At the opposite end of its journey, it lies on the other side of the Sun from the Earth and is fully lit up.

"It is a most beautiful and delightful sight to behold the body of the moon.... It certainly does not possess a smooth and polished surface, but one rough and uneven, and, just like the face of the earth itself, is everywhere full of vast protuberances, deep chasms, and sinuosities."
Galileo.

"The Starry Messenger"

In 1610, Galileo published a book called *The Starry Messenger* in which he documented all his astronomical discoveries.

To flatter his new employer, the Grand Duke Cosimo II, he named Jupiter's moons after him in the text of his new work.

In March 1611, Galileo went to Rome and gave demonstrations of his telescope and delivered lectures on his findings. This was partly to boost interest in his latest book, but it also served as a means of building up a following in support of his anti-Aristotelian views.

Galileo was an exceptional lecturer and captivated audiences with the amazing powers of his wonderful device. Once again his extrovert character and great powers of communication served him well and before long he and his telescope were the talk of Italy. Through the lens of the telescope, the audience could witness for themselves how the Moon looked huge. They could observe the Moon's craters and mountains and see how the

"I have seen stars in myriads, which have never been seen before, and which surpass the old, previously known, stars in number more than ten times. But that which will excite the greatest astonishment by far, and which indeed especially moved me to call the attention of all astronomers and philosophers is this, namely, that I have discovered four planets, neither known nor observed by any one of the astronomers before my time."
Galileo, from "The Starry Messenger".

planets looked so much larger than when seen with the naked eye. Astronomy was no longer a dull subject discussed by intellectuals and professors; suddenly anyone who attended the great scientist's demonstrations could experience its wonders for themselves.

However, support for Aristotle's ideas persisted.

When Galileo returned to Florence in June, he found that a group of philosophers and scientists jealous of his public support and the admiring attitudes of the Grand Duke, had begun to conspire and plot against him. At every turn they argued vehemently against his theories and attacked his work. The battle finally came to a head in 1612 with the publication of a book by a German Jesuit, Christoph Scheiner.

Scheiner had been using telescopes for a year or more. With their help he had observed a number of dark marks on the surface of the Sun. He called these marks sunspots. However, Scheiner was a dedicated Aristotelian and believed that the Sun was unblemished. He proclaimed that the dark spots he had observed were tiny planets orbiting the Sun close to its surface.

When Galileo heard of this he immediately countered by taking his own observations and followed them with a treatise that totally demolished Scheiner's ideas.

Jealousy

And so a fiery dispute began. Scheiner was convinced that he was right and drew on religion and philosophy for support. Galileo made his position clear and came down categorically opposed to Scheiner's views. This put Galileo in a position where it looked as though he was being heretical, turning against Aristotle and the Church.

Then, in December 1614, a further blow came. A young priest, Thomas Caccini, began to preach anti-scientific sermons from his church pulpit. Worse still, he specifically named Galileo as an enemy of the true faith. The fact that Caccini was questioning Galileo's faith came as a particularly painful blow. The scientist had always considered

Opposite: Galileo, aged about forty-six.
Below: Galileo first observed sunspots in 1611.
Top: A sketch he made of his observations.
Bottom: A recent observation of sunspots. This picture represents a distance of some 3,500 miles across.

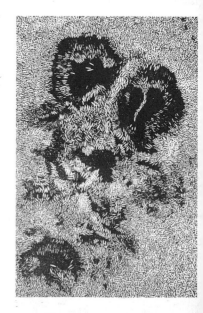

himself a devout Catholic and a true supporter of the faith. He was not questioning God, but the blinkered attitudes of men. He did not see himself as a heretic, but as a thinker who wished to help others out of the darkness of blind faith.

In some ways, Galileo fell into a trap and lost his temper with the Aristotelians. He had always managed to avoid siding publicly with Copernicus. But, at the height of the controversy, he did just that. For once, his charm was not enough to help him. In the short book opposing Scheiner's supporters, he declared his conviction for Copernicus's theory that the Earth was not fixed – it was simply a planet orbiting the Sun.

Within a few months the dispute had come to the notice of the authorities in Rome. By the spring of 1615, much to the delight of his enemies, Galileo had been summoned to Rome to denounce his support for Nicolaus Copernicus.

Galileo was perceived as being dedicated to opposing the Church, who saw him as threatening to the belief systems of future generations. This is a very unfair view of things. Galileo loved the Catholic Church and was an extremely religious man. But, he had strong anti-Aristotelian views. It was the Church who were being irrational. They had claimed it was impossible for Galileo to be a scientist *and* a devout Catholic.

"The Assayer"

When he appeared before the Pope's representative, Galileo withdrew his support for Copernicus and agreed not to teach theories that were sympathetic to these heretical views.

For a while things calmed down. But in 1618, another cosmic event triggered a further round of controversy. Three clearly observable comets appeared in the sky. A Jesuit scientist, Orazio Grassi, claimed that the comets' paths were straight lines and proposed a number of schemes to fit them into the old Aristotelian idea of the Earth being the central point of the universe.

Breaking with the earlier ruling from Rome, Galileo publicly denounced Grassi and the Jesuits

Opposite: An Italian church of the early seventeenth century. Italy is a devoutly religious catholic country today, but in Galileo's day, support for the Roman Catholic Church was at its height. All dissension from the "true faith" was viciously stamped out by the power of the Cardinals and the terror of the Inquisition.

Below: A one-time mathematician and friend of Galileo, Maffeo Barberini. He became Pope Urban VIII in 1623. Galileo expected this appointment to help his case against the narrow-mindedness of the Church, but this was not to be. Barberini put his faith above his scientific side.

By any standards, the Inquisition was terribly cruel and for a religious body, the things they did seem totally at odds with Christian faith. Here you can see prisoners undergoing a variety of horrible tortures at the hands of the Inquisition – all sanctioned by the Pope. Although Galileo was never tortured, the threat of it hung over him throughout the trial.

by writing a book. Called *The Assayer*, it used Copernicus's theory to explain the observed path of the comets.

The comets' courses could be followed by using a telescope. It was clear that their paths were not in fact straight lines, but curved. By applying the most advanced mathematics of the day Galileo was able to show that this fact alone fitted perfectly into Copernicus's scheme and that once more Aristotle had been mistaken.

Unfortunately for Galileo, the authorities decided to totally ignore the evidence and, once more, disagreed with him. As a result, in 1624 the sixty-year-old Galileo was summoned back to Rome.

Persecution

This time the Pope was highly displeased and would not listen to Galileo's opinions. Fortunately, Galileo had built up a lifelong protection for himself. Not only was he a famous and highly-respected scientist, perhaps the greatest of the day, but he had constructed a network of important friends around himself.

His friends spoke out in support of him and managed to appease the angry Pope by persuading Galileo to sign a decree that he would never again teach Copernican ideas. The Pope accepted this. But then came a surprise.

The Pope, Urban VIII, decided that he had heard

"'Sympathy', 'antipathy', 'occult properties', influences, and other terms are employed by philosophers as a cloak for the correct reply, which would be 'I do not know'. That reply is as much more tolerable than the others as candid honesty is more beautiful than deceitful duplicity."
Galileo, from "The Dialogue".

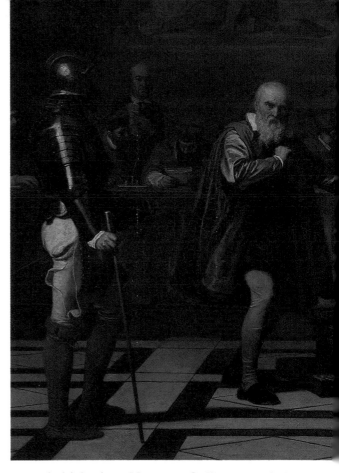

Galileo at his trial in April 1633. He claimed throughout that the "Dialogue" was a balanced account of the two separate philosophies: on the one hand, the work of Ptolemy, based on the thoughts of Aristotle and on the other, the controversial Copernican system. After being advized that a recanting of his pro-Copernican views would save his life, Galileo submitted. With the help of influential friends, he was saved from torture and perhaps even death.

enough bickering. He gave Galileo permission to write a book that would lay out the arguments from both sides of the debate. In this book he was to give a balanced account of the matter. But, that was not the end of the story. Urban made it very clear that the purpose of the book was to end the arguments once and for all – Galileo must finally conclude that the heretical Nicolaus Copernicus was wrong.

Galileo had no choice but to agree to the plan if he was to return to Florence a free man.

Convicted

Nine years after receiving instructions from Rome, Galileo finished his book, *Dialogue Concerning the Two Chief Systems of the World*, and the final storm

broke. Galileo was summoned by the Pope to stand trial for heresy.

Once again in Rome, sixty-nine-year-old Galileo was treated as a criminal. His friends in the hierarchy of the Inquisition undoubtedly saved his life and persuaded the furious Pope to soften the inevitable death sentence to life imprisonment.

Galileo was placed under house arrest. This meant that he was allowed to live in a small house near Florence where he was guarded twenty-four hours a day and was refused permission to travel outside the grounds. His books were totally banned, their sale or distribution punishable by death. His letters to family and friends were censored and visitors had to receive special permission from Rome before they were allowed to talk to the sixty-nine-year-old scientist.

Surviving

At first this terrible treatment took its toll on the great man. He fell into a dark depression that was further deepened by a series of emotional and physical blows.

In 1633 he fell seriously ill, struck down by a recurrence of an infection he had suffered before the trial. The authorities in Rome forbade him to travel to Florence for treatment and the illness grew worse until, at the insistence of friends close to the Pope, he was tended by a visiting doctor.

Then, in 1634, his daughter, Maria Celeste, grew sick and died suddenly in a nearby convent where she had lived as a nun.

Despite these cruel twists of fate Galileo was not beaten. In his old age he returned for a while to his interests outside science. He began to paint again and to play the lute as he had once done as a child. Then, after a while, he regained his burning interest in science and his greatest gifts of curiosity and imagination gradually returned. He began to write again and in his final years he produced lasting and influential discoveries in mechanics.

One of the few concessions the Church authorities made was that he was provided with scientific apparatus and he carried out nightly observations of the Moon, stars and planets with his latest telescope.

Opposite: Although Galileo was a deeply religious man he could not allow catholic dogma to override his scientific training. He knew Copernicus was right. However, he was intelligent enough to realize that if he insisted that the Church was wrong, he would be tortured and could even face an agonizing execution. And for what? The Church would be proven wrong on the matter before long. The world was changing, the scientific revolution would be unstoppable.

"Two New Sciences"

Between 1634 and 1637, in those dark days of captivity, Galileo Galilei produced what many consider to be his greatest scientific work. He called this new book *Two New Sciences*. In it, using the familiar technique of characters discussing the problems involved, he described two important, but very different, areas of science.

In the first half of the book he considered the subject of motion, how objects move and the forces that operate on them. In the second half, he dealt with the properties of matter, and how different materials can be stretched and shaped into various different forms.

"At a very distant date in the future, the average mind may surpass that of Galileo to the same extent as Galileo's surpasses that of a child. And of all the infinite possibilities one may occur to a Galileo of the distant future, which when formulated as a law, may serve to describe motions of a body better than the laws he proposed in 1638."

Albert Einstein.

This final text of Galileo's was truly revolutionary. The first half opened the way for the work of future generations of physicists. The most important of these was the great English genius Sir Isaac Newton who was born the year Galileo died. It is a fascinating fact that Newton's work leads from Galileo's in an almost seamless path, Newton's ideas flowing on from the legacy Galileo left.

Publication

The second half of *Two New Sciences* really was totally new in that no other scientist had ever before considered the properties of materials in a mathematical way. The book suggests theories concerning a variety of things, from why it is that some materials are elastic and others are not, to reasons why only certain substances conduct heat.

Galileo had not lost his touch, in fact, if anything, his genius had matured. The problem was, he was forbidden to have his work published. There was absolutely nothing heretical in this new book, but the declaration from Rome had been all-embracing. Galileo was not allowed to publish a single word, he had been totally silenced. Obviously extreme measures were needed if his work was ever to see the light of day.

With the help of friends, Galileo secretly contacted a company in Holland, a country far enough away from the influence of the Roman Catholic Church to risk the Pope's anger and go ahead with printing the book. The manuscript was smuggled out past the guards and, in 1638, Galileo's greatest work, *Two New Sciences*, was published.

Final days

Galileo worked to the last. Science was in his blood. He lived for discovery, for the excitement of unveiling the secrets of the universe.

In 1637, within weeks of completing *Two New Sciences*, he was struck by a new tragedy. He contracted an eye infection and grew steadily blind, finally losing his sight altogether.

Tuscany has always been a very beautiful part of Europe. In Galileo's time there were very few towns and no industrial areas to spoil the lush green valleys and wooded hills. This was the area in which Galileo spent his youth and to which he returned many times during his life.

He was allowed to employ assistants who carried out scientific observations for him, reporting their findings for the great scientist to analyze and incorporate into his latest theories.

But, Galileo was growing weaker and becoming increasingly resentful of the claustrophobic conditions of his life within the walled grounds.

At the height of winter's chill, on January 8, 1642, Galileo Galilei died in his sleep, finally letting slip his fascination for the world and the processes by which things really worked....

Galileo, a prisoner in his own villa at Arcetri. He was visited by many distinguished people of the time. Beset by tragedy and physical disabilities, Galileo continued to work until the end and produced one of his best books, "Discourses on Two New Sciences", while imprisoned there.

Galileo Galilei's legacy

Viewed as one of the greatest scientists in history, Galileo's work laid the foundation for the development of many branches of science for generations to come. Newton's discoveries in the decades following Galileo's death owe much to Galileo's theories, and astronomy was transformed by his contributions to the design of the telescope.

F Villamena Fac.

What Galileo gave to the world of science is immeasurable. To many he represents the very essence of what the Renaissance meant. He laid the ground work for Newton's pioneering discoveries a generation later. And, in their turn, those principles of motion are still used to this day in every facet of science.

Galileo turned the telescope from a trinket into a scientific instrument of almost unbounded importance. He discovered the concept of acceleration and put the idea into a mathematical form which is used in almost the same way today. He revolutionized our understanding of what happens to objects in free fall and clarified this with simple, meticulous experiments never before imagined. In many ways he was the first real experimental physicist and by example he opened up a whole new approach to science.

However, beyond all these momentous feats, Galileo's greatest contribution was to fight for the position of science in the world. He tried throughout his life to establish clear thinking in science and laid the way for the revolution in human thought which really began a generation after his death, making way for the modern scientific era.

Before Galileo, Europe was an intellectual wasteland, all scientific thought was based on out-moded and naïve ideas that had not changed for two thousand years. After his death, things began to change very quickly thanks to his flawless insight and ceaseless efforts to make the world think.

The antiquated and bigoted religion that had punished Galileo and tried to break his spirit may have dominated and ruled his life, but it never managed to quell his genius.

The Roman Catholic Church completely failed to stem the flow of revolution and the growing enlightenment science brought. Against the clear logic and uncompromising reason of Galileo, the false ideas it clung to were finally swept away.

Thanks to Galileo, the "Age of Enlightenment" very soon began to grow at an unstoppable pace, spreading out across the entire civilized world.

Important Dates

1543   Nicolaus Copernicus's book *The Revolution of the Heavenly Spheres* is published. In the book, Copernicus suggests that Aristotle's theory about the universe is wrong.

1564   Feb 15: Galileo Galilei is born in Pisa, Italy.

1581   Sept: Aged seventeen, Galileo becomes a student at Pisa University.

1583   Galileo begins experimenting with pendulums.

1585   Aged twenty-one, Galileo leaves Pisa University. He continues to study mathematics and begins to give private lessons.

1586   Galileo writes *Il bilancetta*. It brings him to the notice of other scientists and he begins to establish himself as a mathematician.

1589   Galileo, aged twenty-five, is appointed Professor of Mathematics at Pisa University.

1590   Galileo writes *De Motu* which brings together his ideas on motion and falling bodies.

1591   Galileo conducts his experiments from the Leaning Tower of Pisa. Galileo's father dies.

1592   Galileo's contract at Pisa University comes to an end and he is appointed Professor of Mathematics at the University of Padua.
While in Padua, he has a relationship with Marina Gamba and three children are born.

1593   Galileo begins to investigate acceleration using an inclined plane.

1597   The German scientist, Johannes Kepler, publishes *Mysterium Cosmographicum*, which supports Copernicus's theory about the universe.

1604   Galileo proves mathematically that the Earth is not the central point of the universe.
Oct: A supernova appears in the sky, giving Galileo more evidence that Aristotle's theory about the universe is wrong.

1609   Galileo constructs an improved model of the telescope and begins his astronomical observations.

1610   Mar: Galileo publishes *The Starry Messenger*.
Sept: Galileo moves to Florence to take up the position of mathematician to the Grand Duke.

1612   The German Jesuit astronomer, Christoph Scheiner, publishes a book on sunspots. Galileo totally disagrees with Scheiner's reasoning.

1613   Galileo's *History and Demonstrations Concerning Sunspots and their Phenomena* is published. It shows that Galileo supports Copernicus's theory about the universe, not Aristotle's.

1614   Dec: A Dominican priest, Thomas Caccini, condemns Galileo for supporting Copernicus's theory.

1615   Galileo is summoned to Rome to denounce his support for Copernicus.

1618   Three comets appear in the sky, triggering further controversy between Galileo and supporters of Aristotle.

1623 Galileo publishes *The Assayer* in which he challenges the Church's thinking on the universe.

1624 Galileo is told by the Pope to write a "balanced" account of the disagreements between the Church and Copernicus's theory about the universe.

1632 Feb: Galileo's *Dialogue concerning the Two Chief Systems of the World* is published.
Aug: The Church orders the sale of the *Dialogue* to be suspended. The Inquisition summons Galileo to Rome.

1633 April: Galileo, aged sixty-nine, stands trial.
June: Galileo is found guilty. He is given a life sentence and placed under house arrest. The *Dialogue* and all his other works are banned.

1634 April: Galileo's daughter, Marie Celeste, dies.
Galileo begins writing *Discourses and Mathematical Demonstrations concerning Two New Sciences.*

1637 Galileo contracts an eye infection and loses his sight.

1638 *Two New Sciences* is published in Leiden, Holland.

1642 Jan 8: Galileo Galilei dies aged seventy-seven.

Further Reading

Bronowski, J.: *The Ascent of Man*, BBC Books, London.
An adult book that deals with the history of science and technology. It has one chapter devoted to Galileo and shows how his work influenced the progress of western civilization.

Drake, Stillman: *Galileo*, ("Past Masters" series), Oxford University Press.
A scholarly work that deals with the philosophical and religious arguments surrounding Galileo's life rather than the science.

Meadows, Jack (ed.): *The History of Scientific Discovery*, Harrap, London.
A beautiful book dealing with the lives and work of twelve great scientists, including Galileo.

Moore, Patrick: *The Amateur Astronomer*, Cambridge University Press.
The standard handbook for anyone who is interested in astronomy.

Ridpath, Ian: *The Young Astronomer*, Hamlyn, London.
A good introduction to astronomy for younger readers.

Ronan, Colin: *Galileo*, Weidenfeld and Nicholson, London.
A detailed biography of Galileo's life and work, including background information about the Renaissance. It is easy to read, but use the index to browse.

Scientific Terms

Acceleration: In physics, the rate of change of *velocity* with time. Generally, the ability to increase speed.

Area: In *geometry*, the size or extent of a surface measured in squares.

Atom: The smallest particle of a chemical element.

Ballistics: The scientific study of projectiles or missiles moving through the air.

Celestial body: Any object that occurs naturally in space – e.g. a star, planet or comet.

Conduct: In physics, to transmit heat, light, electricity or sound.

Force: An influence that is capable of changing a body's state of rest or uniform motion in a straight line. A force can act from the outside or the inside.

Formula: In mathematics and physics, a statement or law expressed using symbols. In chemistry, symbols that represent the composition of a substance – e.g. H_2O is the chemical formula for water.

Friction: A *force* that resists the movement of one surface against another with which it is in contact.

Geometry: The branch of mathematics concerned with the properties, measurement and relationship of lines, points, angles, surfaces and solids.

Gravity: In physics, a *force* of attraction, acting between two bodies – e.g. between the Earth and bodies near or at its surface.

Mass: The amount of material in an object.

Mechanics: The branch of physics concerned with the study of moving objects and the *forces* acting upon them.

Parabola: In mathematics, a curve formed by a point that moves so that its distance from a fixed point is always the same as its distance from a fixed straight line.

Square root: In mathematics, the square root of a number is another number which, when multiplied by itself, produces the original number – e.g. the square root of 4 is 2, because $2 \times 2 = 4$.

Sunspots: Dark patches that can be seen on the Sun's surface. Their size can range from 2,000km to more than 100,000km. They are thought to be cooler areas on the Sun's surface.

Velocity: The speed at which an object travels in a particular direction.

Volume: In *geometry*, the space taken up by a three-dimensional object.

Index